Betty Crocker's
COOK BOOK
for Boys
and Girls

Copyright © 1957 by General Mills, Inc. Published by Wiley Publishing, Inc. No part of this book may be reprinted in any form or by any means, electronic or mechanical, without permission in writing from the Publisher. Betty Crocker is a registered trademark of General Mills, Inc.
ISBN: 0-7645-2634-0   Manufactured in China
Facsimile Edition 2003   10 9 8 7 6 5 4 3 2 1

We're excited to bring you this treasured edition of *Betty Crocker's Cook Book for Boys and Girls*. All the recipes are exactly as they appeared in the original 1957 book. Some food safety concerns have changed over the years, so please turn to page 192 for today's food safety information.

 WILEY

Dear Boys and Girls,

Cooking is an adventure, as you'll find out when you use these recipes. On the opposite page you can meet the twelve boys and girls who tested the recipes in their own kitchens at home.

It's really easy to cook, once you know how. You'll be trying all sorts of things—Pigs in Blankets, Hot Fudge Pudding, Jolly Breakfast Ring—even a supper for the family some night to give mother a holiday.

If you use your cook book often I can promise you real fun and lots of good things to eat.

Sincerely,

Betty Crocker

Contents

Extra Special

Good things to make for parties—for holidays—for your friends —and just for fun.

Of all the extra-specials, cakes are tops. And how proud you'll be when you make a birthday cake for Dad, a Heart Cake for Mother on Mother's Day, an Igloo Cake for your little sister, or any cake on these pages.

There are lots of other fun things you can make like fancy drinks and Black Cat Cookies and Eggs in a Frame for a camp-fire lunch.

You'll want to try them all before you are through and a good place to start is with a special cake. You can make any of these cakes easily if you follow directions carefully and take to heart all the cakemaking tips over there on the next page.

Meet Our Home Testers

The 12 boys and girls who tested all these recipes

DONNA
"We tested about 136 recipes and we liked almost every one of them."

PETER
"We learned what things mean, like baste and fold and sift."

LUCY
"It's important to measure exactly. When we didn't we had trouble."

ELIZABETH
"All those recipes sound like a lot of work. But we loved it."

CHRIS
"If we didn't like it, Betty Crocker didn't put it in this book."

RANDEE
"Being a home tester was the most exciting thing I ever did."

RICKY
"We always said what we thought, even if it wasn't complimentary."

BECKY
"After all the recipes were tested we had a wonderful party."

LINDA
"Our mother marked what we made excellent, good, fair, or poor."

BETTE ANNE
"We had to say if things were easy or hard and did they taste good."

ERIC
"We had to say if we liked things enough to make them again."

EILEEN
"It's really easy to cook, if you do what it says in the recipe."

COLOR PHOTOGRAPHS

Cakemaking Tips

Liquids and eggs should be about room temperature.

Use a wooden spoon for stirring.

Always prepare cake pans by greasing thoroughly and dusting with flour.

Use a rubber scraper to keep spoon and bowl clean so batter will mix well.

Get the last of the batter out of the bowl with the rubber scraper.

Cake is done when a toothpick stuck into center comes out clean.

When two times are given in the recipe (as 20 to 25 minutes) set timer for first and see if cake is done. Give extra time if needed.

Set pans on cooling racks when they come from the oven.

After 10 minutes turn cake from pans to finish cooling on racks.

Cakes are ready to ice when cool.

Cocoa Fudge Cake

Heat oven to 350°.

Grease and flour 13-inch oblong pan.

Sift together into mixing bowl —
> 1¾ cups *sifted* Gold Medal Flour
> 1⅓ cups sugar
> 1 teaspoon soda
> 1 teaspoon salt
> 6 tablespoons cocoa

Add —
> ½ cup soft shortening
> 1 cup buttermilk
> 1 teaspoon vanilla

Beat vigorously for 2 minutes (300 strokes). You can use an electric mixer if you scrape the sides down often. Use medium speed.

Add —
> 2 eggs

Beat 2 more minutes.

Scrape batter together and be sure it is all blended.

Pour into prepared pan.

Bake *40 to 45 minutes.*

Cool on rack.

Ice, in or out of pan, with Quick Fudge Icing (page 22).

"Baking is as much fun as my chemistry set. And you can eat what you mix up." **Eric**

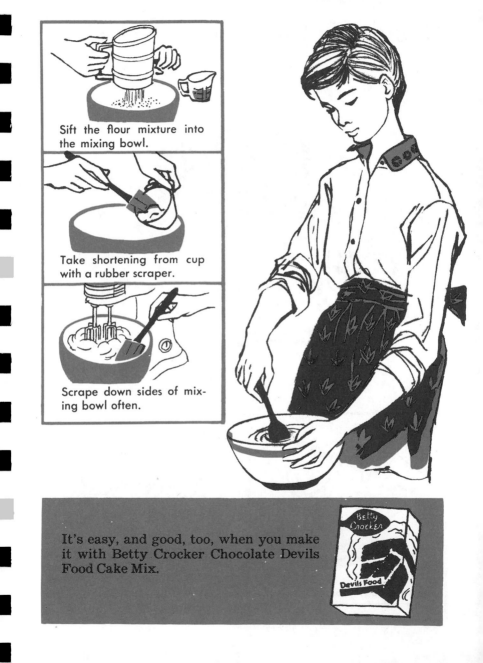

Sift the flour mixture into the mixing bowl.

Take shortening from cup with a rubber scraper.

Scrape down sides of mixing bowl often.

It's easy, and good, too, when you make it with Betty Crocker Chocolate Devils Food Cake Mix.

Grandma's Chocolate Layer Cake

Long ago, a yellow cake with chocolate icing was called a chocolate layer cake.

Break the eggs into a saucer with a kitchen knife.

Use a rubber scraper to clean the sides of the bowl.

Heat oven to 350°.

Grease and flour two 8- or 9-inch round layer pans.

Sift together into mixing bowl ——

> 2¼ cups *sifted*
>   Softasilk Cake
>   Flour
> 1½ cups sugar
> 3 teaspoons
>   baking powder
> 1 teaspoon salt

Add ——

> ½ cup soft
>   shortening
> ⅔ cup milk
> 1½ teaspoons
>   vanilla

Beat vigorously for 2 minutes (300 strokes). You can use an electric mixer if you scrape the sides down often. Use medium speed.

Add ——

> another ⅓ cup
>   milk
> 2 eggs

Beat 2 minutes.

Pour into prepared pans.

Bake *30 to 35 minutes*. Cool.

Finish with Whiz Chocolate Fudge Frosting (page 23).

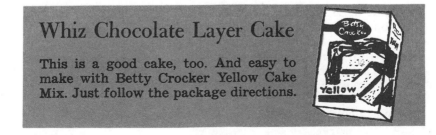

Whiz Chocolate Layer Cake

This is a good cake, too. And easy to make with Betty Crocker Yellow Cake Mix. Just follow the package directions.

Zoo Cake

Bake any flavor Betty Crocker Cake Mix in oblong pan as directed on package.

Frost, using Betty Crocker Fluffy White Frosting Mix, making icing on top about ¼-inch thick.

Press painted or chocolate-coated animal crackers against sides of cake. Fence them in with long gumdrops. Set candles in top of cake. Trim with gumdrops and silver candies.

There is a color photograph of a Zoo Cake on page 38.

To Make Wild Animals for Zoo Cake

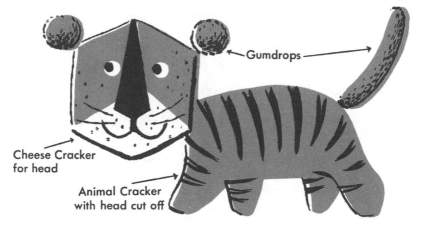

Gumdrops

Cheese Cracker
for head

Animal Cracker
with head cut off

Paint animals with Egg Yolk Paint (page 48).
Bake *3 minutes* at 350° to set egg yolk.

or use chocolate-coated animal crackers (below).

To coat animal crackers:
Melt in custard cup set in hot water and heated ¼ cup semi-sweet chocolate pieces with 1½ tablespoons butter. When chocolate is melted, take from heat and stir with fork until thoroughly blended. Drop crackers, one at a time into chocolate mixture. Lift out with fork, draining off excess, and lay on waxed paper to harden before using.

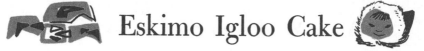

Eskimo Igloo Cake

The Eskimo has his igloo, but no cake like this.

Bake a cake in two layers, as directed on Betty Crocker Chocolate Devils Food Cake Mix package.

Cool thoroughly and cut each layer in half.

Make Betty Crocker Fluffy White Frosting Mix as directed on package.

Spread frosting on one side of three halves. Set halves side-by-side on cut edges with icing between to form a long rounded cake which makes the igloo.

Frost the rounded tops and ends with remaining icing.

Place in custard cup————

> 1 square
>   unsweetened
>   chocolate
>   (1 ounce)
> ¼ teaspoon
>   shortening

Set cup in a little hot water in saucepan. Heat until melted.

There is a color photograph of the Igloo Cake on page 40.

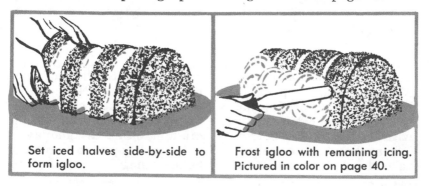

Set iced halves side-by-side to form igloo.

Frost igloo with remaining icing. Pictured in color on page 40.

To make ice blocks on igloo, mark icing into squares by dripping melted chocolate mixture from end of teaspoon.

Clown Cupcakes

Make cupcakes as directed on Betty Crocker Chocolate Devils Food Cake Mix package. Then follow the directions on the opposite page.

"I'm going to make these for my little brother's birthday. Gregg'll be 6." **Chris**

Cut cone-shaped pieces out of tops of cooled, baked cupcakes.

Turn cone-shaped pieces cut-side up for peaked hats.

When ready to serve, fill cavity of each cake with a scoop of vanilla ice cream. Make faces with candies.

Set hats on clown heads. There is a color photograph of Clown Cupcakes on page 73.

Ice Cream Cone Cakes

Heat oven to 400°.

Make batter for cupcakes as directed on any flavor Betty Crocker Cake Mix package.

Pour scant ¼ cup batter into flat-bottomed waffle ice cream cones, filling *scant ½ full.* If you fill the cones too full, they will not have a nice round top.

Set on baking pan and bake *15 to 18 minutes.*

Cool and frost with any Betty Crocker Frosting Mix.

There is a color photograph of Ice Cream Cone Cakes on pages 74 and 75.

"I frosted mine with chocolate fudge frosting and then sprinkled them with those teeny colored candies." **Bette Anne**

Button Cake

Ice your cake with Butter Icing (page 25). Decorate with wafer-thin round candies in different colors.

Draw faces on each with a mixture of

> ¼ cup confectioners' sugar
> 1 teaspoon milk

Icing Makes the Cake

Icing is best when it is as soft as possible, but it must hold its shape without running off the cake.

Spread a little along the inside of the mixing bowl with the back of your mixing spoon and see whether or not it is ready to use or needs more confectioners' sugar or liquid added.

When you are going to ice a layer cake—

Turn one layer upside down on cake plate.

Put on a big spoonful of icing and spread it to the edge of the layer.

Set second layer on, right side up.

Ice the sides, spreading up from bottom to top with knife full of frosting.

Put rest of icing on top and swirl it around to decorate.

"Icing the sides is tricky so I just ice the top. When I get more practice I'll do the sides, too."
Ricky

Quick Fudge Icing

In saucepan mix

> 1 cup sugar
> ¼ cup cocoa

Stir in

> ¼ cup butter
> ½ cup milk
> 2 tablespoons
>   light corn syrup

Bring to boil. Boil for 3 minutes, stirring occasionally.
Take out spoon and set pan in cold water.
When you can hold your hand on the bottom of the pan the syrup is cool enough.

Then stir in

> 1½ cups *sifted*
>   confectioners'
>   sugar
> 1 teaspoon vanilla

You may need

> ½ cup more *sifted*
>   confectioners'
>   sugar

Stir the icing until thick enough to spread. Add more confectioners' sugar or milk if needed.

"This makes dreamy fudge. You just add some more confectioners' sugar ,and half a cup of chopped nuts." **Donna**

Whiz Chocolate Fudge Frosting

It takes only a jiffy when you use Betty Crocker Chocolate Fudge Frosting Mix. You don't even cook it. Just make as directed on the package.

Easy Penuche Icing

Penuche is really candy. It came from Mexico.

In saucepan melt ——————— ½ cup butter

Stir in ———————— 1 cup brown sugar (packed)

Continue cooking over low heat for 2 minutes, stirring.

Stir in ———————— ¼ cup milk

Bring to a full rolling boil, stirring constantly.

Take out spoon and set pan in cold water. When you can hold your hand on the bottom of the pan the syrup is cool enough.

Then stir in ——————— 1¾ to 2 cups *sifted* confectioners' sugar

Set pan in ice water. Beat until thick enough to spread. If icing is too thin, add more confectioners' sugar. If too thick, add a few drops of hot water.

Well-packed brown sugar will hold its shape when turned out of the cup.

A full rolling boil looks like this.

Butter Icing

Blend together
> 1/3 cup soft butter
> 1 cup *sifted*
>   confectioners'
>   sugar
> 1 1/2 teaspoons
>   vanilla
> 3 tablespoons top
>   milk

Then stir in
> 2 cups more *sifted*
>   confectioners'
>   sugar

Beat hard to make the icing fluffy.

Add a little more milk or sugar if you need it to make the icing just right to spread.

Whiz Frostings

They're creamy and smooth. And they almost make themselves because they're so easy with Betty Crocker Instant Frosting Mixes.

Peanut Creme — Especially good with chocolate, spice, or peanut butter cake.

Fluffy White—The whitest, fluffiest icing you ever saw. And easy, too.

Chocolate Malt—If you like malted milks, and who doesn't, you'll love this one.

Chocolate Fudge — Everybody loves fudge flavor, and this is the best.

To make any of these luscious frostings you just follow the directions on the package. And quick as a wink you've made a frosting you're proud of.

Name Cake

This is a cake that will fit anybody's birthday. You can use a Betty Crocker Cake Mix in your favorite flavor, frost it with a light-colored icing, and spell out the name with chocolate pieces.

"I made one for Dad's birthday. It was Chocolate Devils Food with Peanut Créme Icing and Dad said it was keen."

Peter

Funny Bunny Cake

Frost oblong cake with Betty Crocker Chocolate Fudge Frosting Mix.

Cut into squares.

Make marshmallow bunny face on each square piece of cake.

Cut marshmallows in half with scissors and lay flat circles on frosting.

Snip other half of marshmallow for bunny ears.

Draw face with food coloring. Use toothpick dipped in food coloring bottle.

Easter Hat Cake

Easter is a time when every girl wants a new hat. And here's one you can eat.

Mix batter as directed on Betty Crocker Cake Mix package. Bake 9-inch layer for brim and 8-inch layer for crown.

Cut 8-inch layer down to 6-inch size and set on top of 9-inch layer. Frost with Betty Crocker Fluffy White Frosting Mix. Trim with ribbon and tiny flowers.

There is a color photograph of the Easter Hat Cake on page 39.

Cut 6-inch circle of paper. Set on the 8-inch layer. Cut around it with a small knife.

Set 6-inch layer on 9-inch layer near the edge.

You will need a square layer and a round layer.

Cut the round layer in half and place against the square layer.

Heart Cake

A beautiful surprise for Mother's Day, or a Valentine.

Make cake batter as directed on the Betty Crocker White Cake Mix package.

Divide batter between 2 greased and floured pans—one 8-inch square pan, and one 8-inch round layer pan.

Bake as directed on package.

To make heart-shaped cake: Set square cake on large tray with one point toward you. Cut round layer in half. Arrange each half with cut side against top corners of square to form heart.

Frost with Betty Crocker Fluffy White Frosting Mix tinted pink with a few drops of red food coloring. Be sure to cover top of cake well, especially over the cut sections. Decorate with red candies.

There is a color photograph of the Heart Cake on page 39.

"Ned and I love chocolate, so I used chocolate fudge frosting on mine, and it was beautiful!"
Becky

Drum Cake

To celebrate the Fourth of July—make a cake for the family picnic and decorate it for the holiday.

Bake cake in layers as directed on Betty Crocker Chocolate Devils Food Cake Mix package.

Frost cooled cake with Betty Crocker Fluffy White Frosting Mix.

The photograph on the opposite page is of the Drum Cake.

On sides of cake press striped peppermint candy sticks at angles into icing all around cake. Set a maraschino cherry at ends of each stick. If you like, cross two candy sticks on top of cake for drumsticks.

Extra Special Drinks
(see pages 60-63)

Fruit Float

Pink Lemonade

Eggnog

Red Rouser

Chocolate Fudge
Soda

Paintbrush Cookies (see page 48)

Zoo Cake (see page 12)

Heart Cake (see page 30)

Easter Hat Cake (see page 29)

Igloo Cake (see page 14)

Pumpkin Face Cake

Halloween or Thanksgiving, either one rates a special cake.

Bake cake in layers as directed on Betty Crocker Honey Spice Cake Mix package.

Put layers together and frost with Butter Icing (page 25) tinted orange (mix red and yellow food coloring).

Make a Jack-O'-Lantern face with flat black jelly candies and candy corn.

Angel Birthday Cake

Angel Food Cake

Make the cake as directed on Betty Crocker Angel Food Cake Mix package.

Frost it with Betty Crocker Fluffy White Frosting Mix tinted pink with a drop or two of red food coloring.

Li'l Angel Food Cake

A mix just half the size of the big one. Perfect for a tea party or a very small angel's birthday.

Confetti Angel Food Cake

This is the cake with the magic ingredient—hundreds of tiny colored sugar dots. While your cake is in the oven the dots dissolve into rainbow splashes of color.

To make it just follow the package directions.

Lemon Custard Angel Food Cake

Everybody loves this mix, with its new flavor and beautiful sunshine yellow color. Try it as a surprise for Dad.

Fold in and glue together.

Insert tab into cake.

Set on cake at last minute.

Trace this angel on white paper.
Cut it out and put it together.

Black Cat Cookies

Tricky treats for Halloween

Mix thoroughly ————

> ⅓ cup soft
>   shortening
> ⅓ cup sugar
> 1 egg
> ⅔ cup honey
> 1 teaspoon vanilla

Stir in ————

> 2¾ cups *sifted* Gold
>   Medal Flour
> 1 teaspoon soda
> 1 teaspoon salt

Chill.

Heat oven to 375°.

1. Roll dough into balls the size of walnuts. Set on a lightly greased baking sheet.

2. Cover bottom of glass with cloth. Moisten in water, press cookies quickly to flatten and shape into rounds.

3. Bake *about 8 minutes*, or until lightly browned.

4. When cookies come from oven, *at once* set a chocolate peppermint wafer in the center of each cooky.

5. Set 2 chocolate pieces next to mint for head, 1 piece for tail. Lift onto cooling rack as chocolate melts.

6. With toothpick, shape melted chocolate pieces into head and tail on each cooky.

Party Ideas

Paper bag masks are easy to make. Paint on any face you want and cut out holes for the eyes and mouth. You can cut out flaps on the sides for ears.

Make a lantern by cutting slits across a piece of paper, but do not cut all the way to the edges. Then roll your paper in the direction of the slits. Unroll it and roll it in the opposite direction and paste the ends together. Paste on a strip of paper for the handle.

You can decorate your cups, too. When you cut out the figures, fold your paper in half so that both sides will be the same. Paint on any face you want.

Paintbrush Cookies

Mix thoroughly ————

> ⅓ cup soft
>   shortening
> ⅓ cup sugar
> 1 egg
> ⅔ cup honey
> 1 teaspoon vanilla

Stir in ————

> 2¾ cups *sifted* Gold
>   Medal Flour
> 1 teaspoon soda
> 1 teaspoon salt

Chill.

Heat oven to 375°.

Roll dough out on floured pastry cloth, using floured covered rolling pin. Roll to ¼-inch thickness. Cut in different shapes.

Set on greased baking sheet. Paint designs with Egg Yolk Paint. There is a color photograph of these on pages 36 and 37.

Bake *8 to 10 minutes.* For clear colors do not let cookies brown.

Makes 5 dozen 2½-inch cookies.

Egg Yolk Paint

Blend well 1 egg yolk and ¼ teaspoon water. Divide mixture among several small custard cups. Add a different food coloring to each cup to make bright colors. Paint designs on cookies with small paintbrushes. If egg yolk paint thickens on standing, add a few drops of water.

For Unusual Shapes

If you have cooky cutters that you like, you'll use them of course. Always dip them in flour so they won't stick to the dough.

Or make your own patterns— Draw or copy the pattern on heavy cardboard. Cut out each one and grease it. Lay pattern greased side down on dough and cut around it with a sharp knife. Lift onto baking sheet with wide spatula.

Attractive Designs Make the Prettiest Cookies

After you've decided on the shapes, making the design is fun. Try some of these first.

Then let yourself go, use your imagination, and see what exciting designs you can create.

Sugar Cookies

Just the thing with a glass of lemonade.

Heat oven to 400°.

Blend together
> ½ cup shortening
> ½ teaspoon salt
> 1 teaspoon grated lemon rind
> 1 cup sugar

Beat in
> 1 egg, unbeaten
> 2 tablespoons milk

Stir in
> 2 cups *sifted* Gold Medal Flour
> 1 teaspoon baking powder
> ½ teaspoon soda

Drop by rounded teaspoonfuls on lightly greased baking sheet.

Grease bottom of a glass. Dip glass in sugar and flatten each cooky.

Sprinkle cookies with nutmeg.

Bake *8 to 10 minutes,* until light golden.

Cool on a rack.

Makes about 3 dozen cookies.

Drop by rounded teaspoonfuls.

Flatten cooky with glass.

Cool on a rack.

Molasses Crinkles

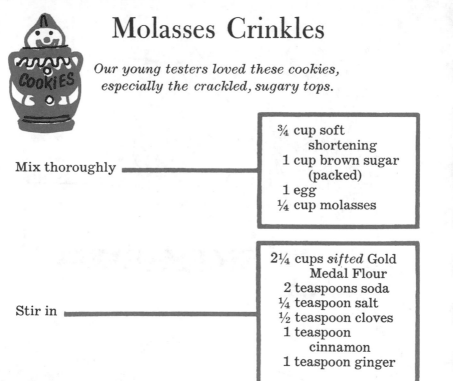

*Our young testers loved these cookies,
especially the crackled, sugary tops.*

Mix thoroughly
—
¾ cup soft
    shortening
1 cup brown sugar
    (packed)
1 egg
¼ cup molasses

Stir in
—
2¼ cups *sifted* Gold
    Medal Flour
2 teaspoons soda
¼ teaspoon salt
½ teaspoon cloves
1 teaspoon
    cinnamon
1 teaspoon ginger

Chill dough.

Heat oven to 375°.

Roll dough into balls the size of large walnuts.

Dip tops in sugar. Place, sugared-side-up, 3 inches apart on greased baking sheet.

Sprinkle each cooky with 2 or 3 drops of water for a crackled surface.

Bake *10 to 12 minutes,* just until set but not hard.

Makes about 4 dozen cookies.

Little sisters like to get in the fun and cook, too.

Roll dough to the size of large walnuts.

Dip tops in sugar.

Whiz Choco-Nut Crinkles

Mix with hands ——————
> 1 package Betty
>   Crocker Yellow
>   Cake Mix
> ¼ cup soft
>   shortening
> 1 medium egg
> 2 tablespoons water

Mix into dough ——————
> 6-ounce package
>   semi-sweet
>   chocolate pieces
> ½ cup chopped nuts

Chill dough.

Heat oven to 375°.

To shape cookies, fill round measuring teaspoon generously, then turn dough out on ungreased baking sheet, round side up.

Place 2 inches apart to allow for spreading.

Bake *about 10 minutes,* until delicately browned. *Do not over-bake.*

Place on cooling rack to crisp.

Makes 3 to 4 dozen cookies.

Good Kid Cookies

Heat oven to 375°.

Empty into bowl ———————— 1 package Betty
                                                       Crocker Marble
                                                       Cake Mix

Take out envelope of marbling mixture to use later.

Add to mix in bowl ———————— 1 egg
                                                 ¼ cup shortening
                                                 2 tablespoons water

Mix thoroughly.

Mix ———————— ¼ cup of the dough
                                                  the envelope of
                                                     marbling
                                                     mixture
                                                 1 tablespoon water

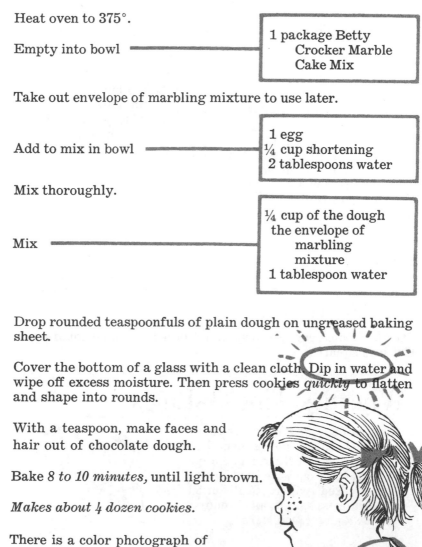

Drop rounded teaspoonfuls of plain dough on ungreased baking sheet.

Cover the bottom of a glass with a clean cloth. Dip in water and wipe off excess moisture. Then press cookies *quickly* to flatten and shape into rounds.

With a teaspoon, make faces and hair out of chocolate dough.

Bake *8 to 10 minutes,* until light brown.

Makes about 4 dozen cookies.

There is a color photograph of
Good Kid Cookies on pages **76** and **77**.

Chocolate Fudge

Mix in saucepan

> 1 cup sugar
> ⅓ cup cocoa

Stir in

> ¼ cup butter
> ¼ cup milk
> 1 tablespoon light
>   corn syrup

Bring to boil. Boil 3 minutes, stirring constantly. Remove spoon and set pan in cold water to cool. When you can hold your hand on bottom of pan, syrup is cool enough.

Stir in

> 3 cups *sifted*
>   confectioners'
>   sugar
> 1 teaspoon vanilla
> ½ cup chopped nuts

Stir until thick enough to spread. Spread in 8-inch square pan Cut into squares.

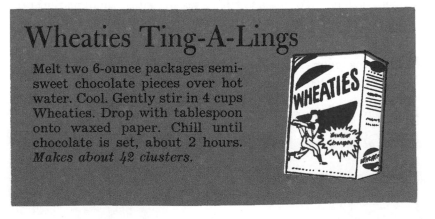

Wheaties Ting-A-Lings

Melt two 6-ounce packages semi-sweet chocolate pieces over hot water. Cool. Gently stir in 4 cups Wheaties. Drop with tablespoon onto waxed paper. Chill until chocolate is set, about 2 hours. *Makes about 42 clusters.*

Peanut Butter Cremes

Beat together

1 well beaten egg*
⅛ teaspoon salt
1 cup *sifted*
    confectioners'
    sugar
½ teaspoon vanilla
1 tablespoon butter
⅓ cup peanut butter

*See p. 192

Then stir in

1 cup more *sifted*
    confectioners'
    sugar

Add more confectioners' sugar if needed to make firm enough to handle. Shape into tiny balls.

Roll each ball in

¾ cup chopped
    salted peanuts

Place on waxed paper and refrigerate to set.

Jet Comets

Stir a 6-ounce package semi-sweet chocolate pieces and ½ cup peanut butter over low heat until chocolate is melted. Pour over 5 cups Sugar Jets in large bowl. Stir gently. Drop onto waxed paper in jet shapes. Chill until hard, 2 hours or overnight. *Makes 60.*

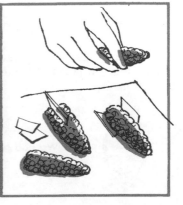

 Taffy

Butter a platter.

Stir together in a large saucepan ——

1 cup sugar
½ cup water
¼ cup light corn syrup
⅛ teaspoon salt

Heat slowly until all sugar is dissolved.

Bring to a boil, stirring constantly.

Continue cooking and stirring. Test occasionally by dropping a small amount from a spoon into a cup of ice water. Taffy is done when you can form a hard ball in the ice water or when it reaches 255° on a candy thermometer.

At once pour onto platter.

When syrup is cool enough to handle, gather it into a ball and pull it until it is white and firm. Grease hands slightly with oil or butter so taffy won't stick to your hands.

Pull taffy out into a rope, twist, and cut with scissors.

Taffy can be flavored by adding a few drops of peppermint, 1 teaspoon vanilla, or 2 tablespoons cocoa just before you start to pull it.

"We had some left over and we wrapped each piece in waxed paper so they wouldn't stick together." **Linda**

Be sure to keep the water ice cold for testing your taffy.

Party Lemonade

In pitcher stir

> ½ cup sugar
> ½ cup hot water

Add

> juice of 2 to 3
>   lemons
> ½ lemon, sliced very
>   thin
> 1 quart cold water
> 12 ice cubes

Stir vigorously with a wooden spoon and pour into tall glasses.

4 servings.

Pink Lemonade

Add a drop of red food coloring to Party Lemonade.

Fruit Float

Pile fruit (raspberries, blueberries, banana slices, strawberries, or any fruit you like) in tall glass. Fill with lemonade or fruit juice and top with lime ice.

"We had a circus party with pink lemonade and clown cupcakes." **Randee**

Eggnog

So good when you're hungry after school.

Beat with rotary beater ————
| 1 egg, well beaten* |
| 2 tablespoons sugar |
| pinch of salt |

*See p. 192

Then beat in ————
| 1 cup cold milk |
| ¼ teaspoon vanilla |

Add ————
| 1 cup cracked ice |
| (see page 62) |

Pour into two glasses.

Sprinkle lightly with nutmeg.

Red Rouser

Drop a scoop of vanilla ice cream into a tall glass. Fill with bottled cranberry juice.

There are color photographs of some of these drinks on pages 34 and 35.

Chocolate Fudge Milk Shake

Make Chocolate Sauce as directed on Betty Crocker Chocolate Fudge Frosting Mix package.

Put in shaker — ½ cup Chocolate Sauce
2 cups milk
pinch of salt
1 cup cracked ice

Shake vigorously
2 servings.

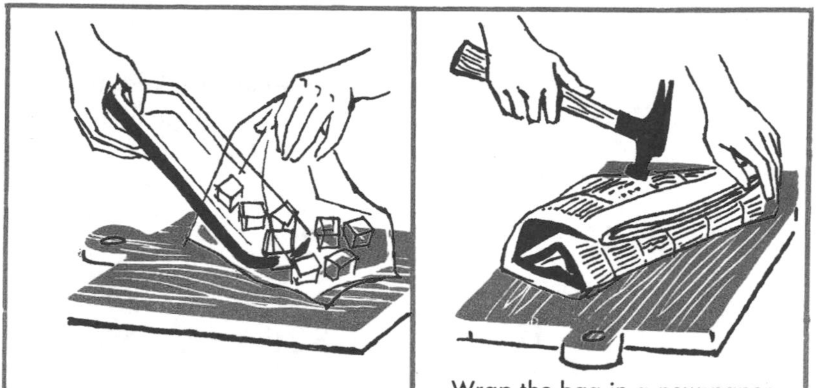

To crack the ice, drop the cubes into a small plastic bag.

Wrap the bag in a newspaper and pound it with a rolling pin or a hammer.

A glass jar with a screw top makes a very good shaker.

Chocolate Fudge Soda

*Why go to the drug store? You can
make your own sodas at home.*

Make Chocolate Sauce as directed on Betty Crocker Chocolate
Fudge Frosting Mix package.

Mix in large glass _____

> 2 tablespoons
>   Chocolate Sauce
> ¼ cup carbonated
>   water

Add _____

> 1 to 2 large scoops
>   vanilla ice
>   cream

Pour in _____

> ¼ cup more
>   carbonated
>   water

Stir to blend slightly and serve at once.

Campfire Cooking

When you cook outdoors it's a good idea to appoint one of the group Chief. The Chief can then give everyone a job to do.

Travel Light. Don't take more equipment than you need. Extra things to carry are just a burden. A frying pan, pancake turner, empty coffee can, stirring spoon, small pail for water, a sharp knife, and a fork for everyone will be enough for any of the recipes given to you here.

Building the Fire. The Hunter's Fire is easy and gives a steady heat. To build it, lay 2 green logs in a V-shape, about 7 inches apart at one end and 4 inches apart at the other. The wider opening should face the wind.

Build a foundation fire between the logs and then add fuel as you need it. For the best results, you should let the fire burn down to coals before you start to cook.

When you are ready to cook, set the frying pan near the narrow end.

Don't Play With Fire. Small fires are the best. They're the easiest to work with and they don't get away from you.

Keep a pail of water handy for putting out the fire. If you don't have water, sand will do the trick.

Before you leave the camp site, be sure your fire is out and the ground completely cold.

Eggs in a Frame

Picnic Lunch in the Woods
Eggs in a Frame
Pocket Salad
(cleaned radishes, celery,
and carrot sticks in plastic
bags to carry in your pocket)
S'mores (page 72)

Pull center from a slice of bread, or cut out center with biscuit cutter.

Butter bread generously on both sides.

Brown bread "frames" on one side in moderately hot buttered frying pan. Turn over.

Drop egg into center.

Cook slowly until egg white is set. (Cover pan until white starts to set.)

Sprinkle lightly with salt.

Lift out with pancake turner.

You can make Eggs in a Frame at home like the color photograph on page 80.

Butter-Fried Potatoes

Take to your picnic 6 medium-sized boiled potatoes cooked in their skins and diced.

In frying pan melt ——————

> ½ stick butter
> (¼ cup)

Add to butter ——————

> 6 medium-sized
>   boiled potatoes,
>   diced
> 1 onion, minced

Sprinkle in ——————

> ¼ teaspoon salt
> 2 tablespoons
>   minced parsley

Cook over a medium-hot campfire until potatoes brown on the bottom. Then lift with pancake turner and brown the other side of the potatoes.

4 to 6 servings.

Soap the entire outside of your frying pan before using it over a campfire. Then the smoke washes off without scouring.

Make a skewer from a green stick as thick as a lead pencil. Sharpen the thin end.

Cut into 1-inch pieces	¼ pound beef sirloin
Cut in half and peel	1 onion
Cut in half	1 tomato

Push the meat, onion, and tomato alternately on the stick. Or, try an apple instead of tomato for variety.

Broil by holding close to hot coals, turning constantly. Cook until meat is brown and vegetables are tender.

Makes 1 kabob for 1 dinner.

There is a color photograph of Kabobs on page 78.

Mulligan Stew

In small amount of hot fat in heavy frying pan, brown —— 1 pound stew meat, cut in small pieces

Add —— 1 teaspoon salt

Stir in —— 1 can condensed tomato soup
1 can water

Cover tightly and let cook slowly until tender (about 1½ hours). If fire gets too hot, take from heat occasionally to keep at a simmer.

When meat is tender, add —— 3 carrots, cut in thick slices
3 potatoes, quartered
3 onions, halved

Continue cooking slowly about 30 minutes. If there is not enough juice, add water during cooking. If too thin take off lid and cook sauce until thickened.

4 to 6 servings.

Doughboys

Make biscuit dough by following directions on Bisquick package for Biscuits.

Dip your hands in Bisquick and pick up a small piece of dough. Roll between the palms of your hands to shape a ribbon about 5 inches long and the size of your little finger.

Heat a peeled green stick over the fire (willow is good for this).

Wind a ribbon of dough spirally around the stick, pinching tightly at each end to hold it onto the stick.

Toast over hot coals, turning to bake evenly. With a good bed of coals Doughboys bake in just a few minutes and slip easily off the stick.

Eat with jam or butter.

There is a color photograph of Doughboys on page 79.

Make tiny rolls no bigger than your little finger.

Wind the dough around the stick like this.

"A coffee can makes the best mixing bowl in camp, cause you can throw it away when you're through." **Elizabeth**

Whiz Doughboys

They're twice as easy with refrigerated biscuits, ready to bake. You know, the kind that come in a can, either Bisquick or Puffin.

Scout Franks and Beans

Into a heavy frying pan empty —
| 1 no. 300 can baked beans (1 pound) |

Top with —
| 8 franks, sliced |

Set over coals and heat until steaming hot.

4 to 6 servings.

S'mores

They got this name because they make you want some more.

You will need —
| graham crackers
marshmallows
milk chocolate bar |

Set 4 squares of a milk chocolate candy bar on a graham cracker.

Toast a marshmallow over the coals of your campfire. Slip it onto the chocolate and top with a second graham cracker.

Clown Cupcakes (see page 16)

Ice Cream Cone Cakes (see page 18)

Good Kid Cookies
(see page 55)

Doughboys (see page 70)

Kabobs (see page 78)

Eggs in a Frame (see page 66)

Branded Pancakes (see page 89)

Breakfast

*Make it the best meal of the day—
a happy family get-together.*

You can be a big help. In one family we know, everyone takes a turn helping to get breakfast. And what rivalry!

The littlest one pours out the cereal, puts the silver around, or rings the breakfast bell.

Older children choose their jobs—fixing the fruit, adding fancy touches to the cereal, frying the eggs, stirring up an easy coffee cake, making cocoa.

Make pancakes for Dad with his initials on them (page 89). Or give your mother a holiday and prepare breakfast all yourself.

Toast Toppers

Everybody loves crisp, hot buttered toast, even more when it's topped with something sweet or spicy.

Orange Sugar

Blend 1 tablespoon soft butter and 3 tablespoons sifted confectioners' sugar. Stir in 1 teaspoon grated orange rind and 1 teaspoon orange juice. Spread on unbuttered toast. Cut in half crosswise.

Cranberry

Spread hot toast with cranberry jelly. Sprinkle with confectioners' sugar.

Cinnamon Mix

Combine 1 teaspoon cinnamon and 2 tablespoons sugar. Sprinkle on hot buttered toast. Cut in strips.

Raisin Peanut Butter

Mix ¼ cup crunchy peanut butter, 2 tablespoons chopped seedless raisins, 2 tablespoons orange juice. Spread on hot toast. Cut in 3 diagonally.

Caramel Coconut

Blend 1 tablespoon soft butter, 2 tablespoons brown sugar, and 2 tablespoons of flaked coconut. Spread on unbuttered toast and toast under broiler until it bubbles. Watch carefully.

Breakfast Treats

What is breakfast without fruit? Orange juice, sliced bananas, and berries are everyday favorites. But have you ever thought of combining different fruits to add zip to the morning? You might start with these and then invent some combos of your own.

Polka Dot Day-Brightener: Raisins sprinkled on applesauce

A Taste of Hawaii: Strawberries and pineapple chunks

Fourth of July Firecracker: Blueberries and raspberries

Tropical Morning: Sliced bananas in orange juice

Peach Melba: Raspberries and sliced peaches

Real Cool Combo: Just-thawed frozen strawberries and seedless grapes

Easy and Good

Orange Juice
Kix with Milk
French Toast (page 85)
with Syrup and Butter
(heated together)
Cocoa Continental (page 84)

A Cheery Breakfast

Cheerios sprinkled
over Pink Applesauce (page 133)
Fried Eggs, Sunny Side Up
Cinnamon Muffins (page 100)
Milk

Summer Holiday Special

Wheaties and Softened Ice Cream
topped with Frozen Strawberries
Hot Buttered Toast Strips
with Bright Jelly
Cold Milk

Cocoa Continental

Blend in saucepan

> 2 tablespoons cocoa
> 3 tablespoons sugar
> ⅛ teaspoon salt

Then stir in

> ½ cup hot water

Bring to boil over low heat and boil
2 minutes, stirring constantly.

Then add and heat, but *do not boil*

> 2 cups milk *or* 1 cup
> evaporated milk
> and 1 cup water

Drop a marshmallow into each cup and pour hot cocoa over it.

4 servings.

French Toast

With beater blend

2 eggs, beaten
½ cup milk
¼ teaspoon salt

Cut in half

6 slices stale bread

Heat frying pan or griddle moderately hot. Grease with butter or bacon fat.

Pick up bread on fork, by half-slices. Dip both sides into egg mixture and put on hot frying pan or griddle.

Brown on both sides, turning with pancake turner.

Serve hot with syrup or jelly.

Soft-Cooked Eggs

Never boil eggs. Always cook them slowly and gently.

Cover eggs in saucepan with cold water. Heat until water boils.

Take from heat. Cover pan. Stand *off heat* 2 to 4 minutes.

Take from hot water. Hold the egg with a paper napkin and break shell by cracking sharply with a knife. Scoop egg from shell with a teaspoon.

Season with salt and butter.

Break soft-cooked eggs by cracking sharply with a knife.

Fried Eggs

Heat a thin layer of butter or bacon fat in heavy frying pan until moderately hot.

Break eggs, one at a time, into saucer. Slip into frying pan.

Reduce heat to cook slowly. Cover and cook until whites are set (3 or 4 minutes).

You can turn the eggs if you like them that way. Then cook until yolks are as you want them.

It's easier to keep the yolks whole if you slip the eggs one at a time from a saucer into the frying pan.

Scrambled Eggs

Break into bowl ━━━━━━━━━━ | 2 eggs

Add ━━━━━━━━━━ | 2 tablespoons milk
dash of salt

Beat with fork.

Heat a thin layer of butter or bacon fat in small moderately hot frying pan.

Pour in egg mixture and reduce heat to low. Cook slowly, turning gently with broad spatula as mixture starts to set at bottom of pan.

Serve as soon as eggs are cooked through but still moist and shiny.

1 or 2 servings.

Pancakes

Grandma called pancakes flannel cakes because on cold mornings they kept her family warm as flannel.

Branded Pancakes

Real Western with your own brand right on the pancake.

Make Pancakes as directed on Bisquick package.

Let batter trickle from teaspoon onto hot griddle to form an initial. Initials must be made backwards to be right when pancakes are served. Draw your initial backwards on a piece of paper for a pattern before you start.

This is how some letters look backward.

When bottom side of initial has lightly browned, pour a regular spoonful of batter over initial.

Bake until bubbles appear, then turn and finish baking as directed on package.

Serve hot with butter and warm syrup or jelly. There is a color photograph of Branded Pancakes on page 80.

Put a very little batter in your spoon when making the initials.

"My 3 brothers can sure eat a lot of pancakes, especially when they're branded." **Lucy**

Dollar Pancakes

Add a little more milk (about ¼ cup) than usual to make pancake batter thin (recipe on Bisquick package).

Then spoon batter, a tablespoon at a time, to fill your griddle with tiny "dollar" pancakes.

Bake as for other pancakes.

Serve several at a time on each plate.

Make sure you keep the pancakes small.

Rolled Pancakes

Spread warm small pancakes (recipe on Bisquick package) with shimmering red jelly. Roll up.

Sprinkle with confectioners' sugar.

Serve two on each individual dessert plate.

Spread jelly thin.

This is how they look rolled up.

Tricks and Treats
with Cereals

You'd be surprised how much more exciting breakfast can be if you try something different every day. Just watch your little brother's face when you surprise him with the Little Man Who Wasn't There or A Pig in a Poke. Or, just put softened ice cream and strawberries over a big bowl of Wheaties. You'll find color photographs of some of these treats on pages 118 and 119.

Man in the Moon

Here he is in a bowl of Cheerios. You make his face with raisins. Or you can make any face you like.

Winken, Blinken, and Nod

3 maraschino cherries sitting in half a banana, an apple slice for a sail, on Trix.

Pig in a Poke

Half pear on Sugar Jets—raisin eyes and nose, apple slices for ears.

Little Man Who Wasn't There

Half banana in Kix, raisin eyes and nose, cherry mouth, orange hat.

Fatso

Half peach on Cheerios, raisin eyes, maraschino cherry nose, apple slice for mouth.

Old Black Joe

Prune on Wheaties, bits of apple for eyes, mouth, ears. Banana and cherry hat.

Easy Coffee Bread

In mixing bowl put ————

> ¾ cup warm (not hot) water
> 1 package active dry yeast

Stir until yeast is dissolved.

Then stir in ————

> ¼ cup sugar
> 1 teaspoon salt
> 1 cup *sifted* Gold Medal Flour

Beat 2 minutes.

Next add ————

> 1 egg
> ¼ cup soft shortening

Beat in until smooth ————

> 1¼ cups *sifted* Gold Medal Flour

Then add ————

> ½ cup raisins

Grease an 8 or 9-inch square pan.

Drop small spoonfuls over entire bottom of pan. Cover.

Let rise in warm place (85° is best) until dough is double in bulk. This takes about 60 minutes. *Be sure dough has risen before baking.*

Heat oven to 375°.

Bake *30 to 35 minutes,* or until lightly browned.

Take from pan immediately to avoid sticking.

Easy Coffee Bread Icing

When bread is baked, ice with a mixture of

¾ cup *sifted* confectioners' sugar
1 or 2 tablespoons orange juice
¼ teaspoon grated orange rind

Drop dough in small spoonfuls

Grate only outside colored rind of orange, no white.

Jolly Breakfast Ring

It looks like a Christmas wreath.

Heat oven to 400°.

Melt ———————————— | 4 tablespoons butter (½ stick)

Put 2 tablespoons of the melted butter in bottom of 9-inch ring mold.

Then sprinkle in ———————— | 2 tablespoons brown sugar
12 cherries (candied or maraschino)
¼ cup chopped nuts

Mix in small bowl ———————— | ½ cup sugar
1 teaspoon cinnamon
3 tablespoons chopped nuts

In second small bowl put ———— | 2 cups Bisquick

With fork stir in ———————— | ⅔ cup milk

Beat 15 strokes. It will be stiff, but sticky.

Shape dough into 12 balls. Roll each ball in rest of melted butter. Then roll in cinnamon mixture. Place balls in ring mold.

Bake *25 to 30 minutes.*

Turn upside down onto a plate while warm. Serve warm. There is a color photograph of Jolly Breakfast Ring on page 116.

Hold point of knife against cutting board.

Chop through nuts, swinging handle slowly as you chop.

Roll balls of dough first in butter, then cinnamon mixture.

Set balls close together in ring mold.

Gingerbread

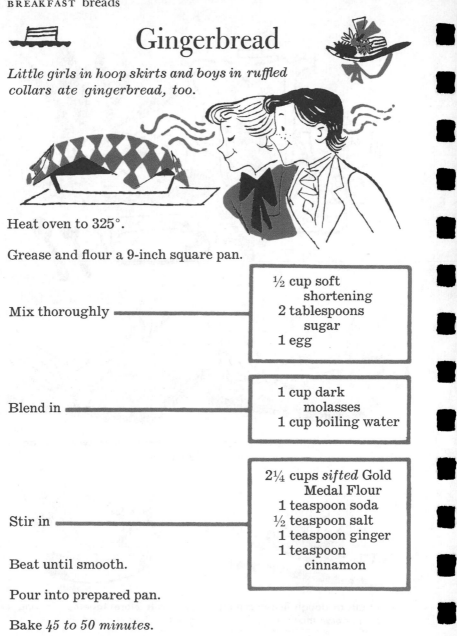

Little girls in hoop skirts and boys in ruffled collars ate gingerbread, too.

Heat oven to 325°.

Grease and flour a 9-inch square pan.

Mix thoroughly ————
| ½ cup soft shortening |
| 2 tablespoons sugar |
| 1 egg |

Blend in ————
| 1 cup dark molasses |
| 1 cup boiling water |

Stir in ————
| 2¼ cups *sifted* Gold Medal Flour |
| 1 teaspoon soda |
| ½ teaspoon salt |
| 1 teaspoon ginger |
| 1 teaspoon cinnamon |

Beat until smooth.

Pour into prepared pan.

Bake *45 to 50 minutes.*

Fire Dog Topping

Spread over hot gingerbread a mixture of ————

³⁄₄ cup *sifted*
     confectioners'
     sugar
2 tablespoons milk

Sprinkle brown sugar over top. Serve warm.

Whiz Gingerbread

For this delicious quickie, make as directed on Betty Crocker Gingerbread Mix package.

"You'll love this gingerbread with a dish of icy-cold applesauce." **Betty Crocker**

Whiz Cinnamon Rolls

Sweet and spicy, and so pretty.

Heat oven to 425°.

Grease 12 muffin cups.

Beat 15 strokes with fork ——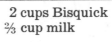

| 2 cups Bisquick |
| ⅔ cup milk |

Roll dough around on cloth-covered board lightly dusted with Bisquick to prevent sticking.

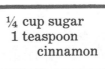

Knead gently 8 to 10 times to smooth up dough.

Roll into 12x7-inch rectangle.

Spread with soft butter.

Sprinkle with mixture of ——

| ¼ cup sugar |
| 1 teaspoon |
| cinnamon |

Roll up tightly widthwise. Seal well.

Cut into 1-inch slices.

Set in muffin cups.

Bake *about 15 minutes,* or until brown.

Makes 12 rolls.

Your dough will be stiff and sticky after beating it with fork.

Roll dough on floured, cloth-covered board.

Knead dough by pressing, folding, and turning.

Roll from the long end of the rectangle.

Set in muffin cups.

Cinnamon Muffins

Heat oven to 400°.

Grease 12 medium-sized muffin cups.

In bowl blend with a fork ———

> 1 egg
> 2 tablespoons
>   sugar
> ¾ cup milk
> 2 cups Bisquick

Beat hard 30 seconds. The batter will be lumpy.

Fill muffin cups ⅔ full.

Stir together ———

> ½ cup brown sugar
> 1½ teaspoons
>   cinnamon

With a teaspoon sprinkle cinnamon and sugar mixture over muffin tops.

Bake *about 15 minutes,* or until golden brown.

Serve hot.

Makes 12 medium-sized muffins.

Whiz Muffins

Four different flavors—orange, date, raisin bran, and corn, each in its own package. Make them with Betty Crocker Muffin Mix.

Lunch or Supper

LUNCH—usually at noon.

SUPPER—at night if dinner is at noon.

Both are light meals—and simple—a good place for the new cook to start learning to do a few things well . . . A perfect hamburger . . . Cheese Dreams . . . Angel Food Cake . . . Hot Fudge Pudding . . . Oatmeal Cookies.

There are lots of other good things, too, that you'll want to try. One day it might be Tuna Burgers or Raggedy Ann Salad. Another day you could try Pigs in Blankets or Applesauce Cake.

First thing you know you'll be getting a complete lunch or supper for your mother when she's very busy.

When You Set the Table

It's easy if you remember to place the silver in the order you're going to use it, with the piece to be used first on the outside, farthest from the plate. That's why the soup spoon is on the outside. Forks and napkins are always at the left and knife, spoons, and glasses at the right.

Saturday Lunch
Cream of Tomato Soup
Bunny Salad (page 127)
Peanut Butter Sandwiches
Fruit Gelatin (page 132)
Milk

Tuna Burgers

Cut the cheese into small, square pieces.

Mix in bowl ——————

| one 7-ounce can tuna |
| 1 cup chopped celery |
| ½ cup diced process yellow cheese |
| 1 small onion, minced |
| ¼ cup mayonnaise |
| salt and pepper to taste |

Split and butter ——————

6 hamburger buns

Fill buns with tuna mixture and replace tops.

Heat in paper sandwich bags on baking sheet at 350° for *15 minutes.*

"We had them for Sunday supper. I made them in the morning, put each one in a waxed paper bag, and left them in the refrigerator. Then we just heated them at supper time." **Donna**

Hamburgers

Mix thoroughly ———

> 1 pound ground beef
> ½ cup evaporated milk
> 1 teaspoon salt

Form into 4 thick or 8 thin patties.

Place on broiler rack or small pan 3 inches from heat. Broil about 6 minutes on each side for medium done hamburgers. (Cook until done to your taste.)

4 servings.

Cheeseburgers

Top the meat with a slice of cheese before you broil it. Make a face with olives and cheese.

Double-Deckers

Cut the unsliced bun in 3 slices. Put your hamburger in the first layer, then pickle relish and sliced tomato in the top layer.

There is a color photograph of Cheeseburgers and Double-Deckers on pages 114 and 115.

Open-Faced Hamburgers

Mix thoroughly ——————

> ¼ cup evaporated milk
> ½ slice soft bread, pulled in pieces
> ½ teaspoon salt
> 1 teaspoon grated onion
> ½ pound ground beef

Stir vigorously to blend.

Place on rack under broiler ——————

> 4 slices bread

Spread hamburger on with a rubber scraper.

Toast bread on one side and spread hamburger mixture on untoasted sides. Be sure to cover the edges.

Return to broiler rack and broil until hamburger is done, *5 to 10 minutes.*

"It's easier to cut the onion up real fine than grating it, so that's what I did." Ricky

Saucy Hamburger Crumble

Melt in frying pan	1 tablespoon fat
Add and brown lightly	1 small onion, chopped
Then add and brown	1 pound ground beef 1 teaspoon salt

Break the meat into small pieces.

Stir in	¼ cup Gold Medal Flour
Then stir in	2 cups water or milk

Heat until gravy bubbles.

Serve over mashed potatoes.

4 servings.

Family Supper
Saucy Hamburger Crumble
on Mashed Potatoes
Candle Salad (page 126)   Crusty Rolls
Whiz Applesauce Cake (page 134)   Milk

Sloppy Joes

*Here you're strictly on your own. Pour in a lot of cat-
sup and a little soup or the other way around. Toss in
some chopped pickle if you have it. Eat it on buns.*

You will need

ground beef
catsup
tomato soup
hamburger buns

Brown the meat and crumble it with a fork. Stir in catsup and
tomato soup. Heat until it bubbles. Serve in buns.

Movie Night Supper

Sloppy Joes
Carrot Curls, Celery Sticks,
Radish Roses (page 142)
Brownies (page 140)
Milk

"If I were a mama, I'd cook all day."   **Elizabeth**

Toasted Cheese-Bacon Sandwiches

Place on rack under broiler

4 slices bread
8 slices bacon

Toast bread on one side and take from rack.

Broil bacon until crisp.

Stir together

1 egg, slightly beaten
¾ cup grated American process cheese
¼ teaspoon paprika
½ teaspoon Worcestershire sauce

Spread mixture over untoasted side of bread. Broil until cheese melts.

Serve with 2 strips of bacon on each slice. Serve at once.

4 servings.

"I mixed the cheese and egg with the rubber scraper. And spread it on the bread that way too. It was real quick and easy." **Eric**

Egg Salad Sandwich Rolls

Mix together ———

> 3 hard-cooked eggs, chopped
> ¼ cup finely chopped celery
> ½ teaspoon minced onion
> 3 tablespoons mayonnaise
> ¼ teaspoon salt

With fork, scoop centers from ———

> 4 sliced frankfurter rolls

Fill each roll with egg salad.

Makes 4 sandwich rolls.

Hard-Cooked Eggs

Cover eggs in saucepan with cold water. Heat until water boils.

Take pan from heat. Cover. Let stand *off heat* 23 to 25 minutes.

Set saucepan in sink and run in cold water to cool the eggs quickly. This makes eggs easier to shell and keeps yolks from turning dark around the edges.

Clean the bowl well with a rubber scraper.

Macaroni and Cheese

An old favorite, as old as Yankee Doodle.

Heat oven to 350°.

Prepare 8-ounce package macaroni
as directed on package.

Combine ——————

> cooked macaroni
> 2 tablespoons
>   butter, cut in
>   pieces
> 1¼ cups cubed
>   sharp cheese
> 1 teaspoon salt

Turn into greased 1½-quart (large)
baking dish.

Blend together ——————

> 2 eggs, beaten
> 3 cups milk

Pour milk and egg mixture over macaroni.

Sprinkle with paprika.

Bake *40 to 50 minutes.*

6 servings.

"Betty Crocker told me a slick way to measure
the butter. She says there are 8 tablespoons in
a ¼-pound stick, so ¼ of a stick is 2 tablespoons."
Eileen

Pigs in Blankets

Heat oven to 450°.

Make Rolled Biscuits as directed on Bisquick package.

Roll dough about ¼-inch thick into rectangular shape.

Cut into 4x3-inch oblongs.

Wrap each oblong around a wiener, letting ends of wiener peep out.

Bake *15 minutes*. Serve hot.

Makes 12.

The color photograph of Pigs in Blankets is on opposite page.

There are two kinds of hot dogs
  The wiener—
    short and skinny
  The frankfurter—
    long and plump

Sloppy Joes (see page 107)

Double-Deckers (see page 104)

Cheeseburgers (see page 104)

Jolly Breakfast Ring (see pages 94-95)

Easy Coffee Bread (see page 92)

Whiz Cinnamon Rolls (see pages 98-99)

118

Cereal Tricks (see pages 90-91)

Grilled Cheese Sandwich

Butter generously ———————— 2 slices bread

Between slices,
buttered-side-out, put ———————— 1 slice American
process cheese

Brown lightly on both sides in frying pan or on griddle over
moderate heat until cheese melts.

Cheese Dreams

Place on rack under broiler ————————
3 English muffins,
split in half and
buttered
6 slices bacon, cut in
half

Toast muffins on one side
and take from rack.

Broil bacon until crisp.

Top each muffin half with ————————
thick tomato slice
2 broiled bacon
strips
thin slice of
processed cheese

Return to broiler and broil 5 inches from heat until cheese
melts.

Serve at once. *6 servings.*

There is a color photograph of Cheese Dreams on opposite page.

Creamed Dried Beef

Melt in heavy frying pan —————— ¼ cup butter

Add and cook a few minutes ————— 4 ounces dried beef, shredded

Blend in ——————————————— ¼ cup Gold Medal Flour

Stir thoroughly. Take from heat.

Add and blend —————————————— 2 cups milk

Heat to boiling, stirring constantly.

To Bake Potatoes

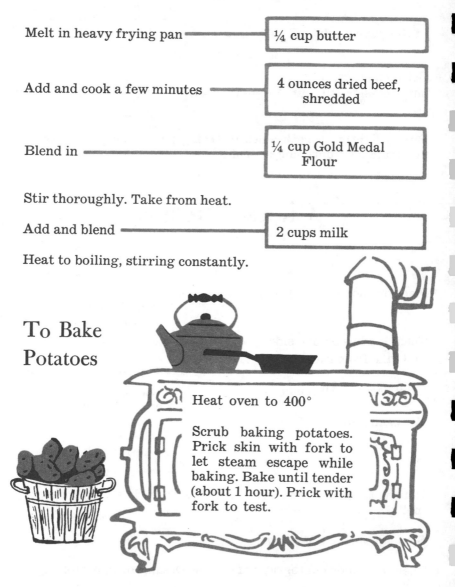

Heat oven to 400°

Scrub baking potatoes. Prick skin with fork to let steam escape while baking. Bake until tender (about 1 hour). Prick with fork to test.

Three Men in a Boat

Hollow out part of a baked potato so it looks like a boat.

Fill the hollow with creamed dried beef.

Cut a sail from a firm slice of cheese and stand upright in the boat on a toothpick.

Three mushrooms on edge of potato "boat" are "3 men."

There is a color photograph of Three Men in a Boat on p.159.

Salad Tips

When you make a salad always use cold ingredients and then chill the finished salad before you serve it. Lettuce makes a pretty garnish that's good to eat and everyone will want to eat it if it's fresh and crisp.

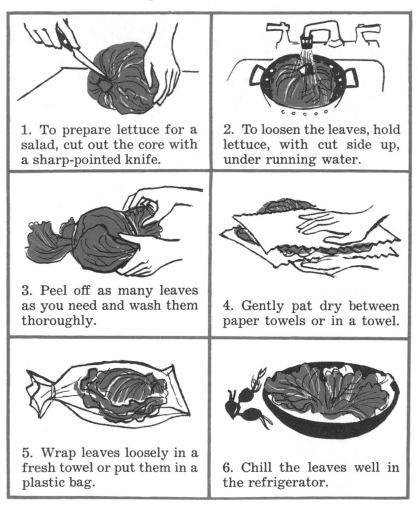

1. To prepare lettuce for a salad, cut out the core with a sharp-pointed knife.

2. To loosen the leaves, hold lettuce, with cut side up, under running water.

3. Peel off as many leaves as you need and wash them thoroughly.

4. Gently pat dry between paper towels or in a towel.

5. Wrap leaves loosely in a fresh towel or put them in a plastic bag.

6. Chill the leaves well in the refrigerator.

Raggedy Ann Salad

Body	fresh or canned peach half
Arms and legs	small celery sticks
Head	half a hard-cooked egg
Eyes, nose, shoes, buttons	raisins
Mouth	piece of a cherry or a redhot
Hair	grated yellow cheese
Skirt	ruffled leaf lettuce

There is a color photograph of Raggedy Ann Salad on page 158.

Candle Salad

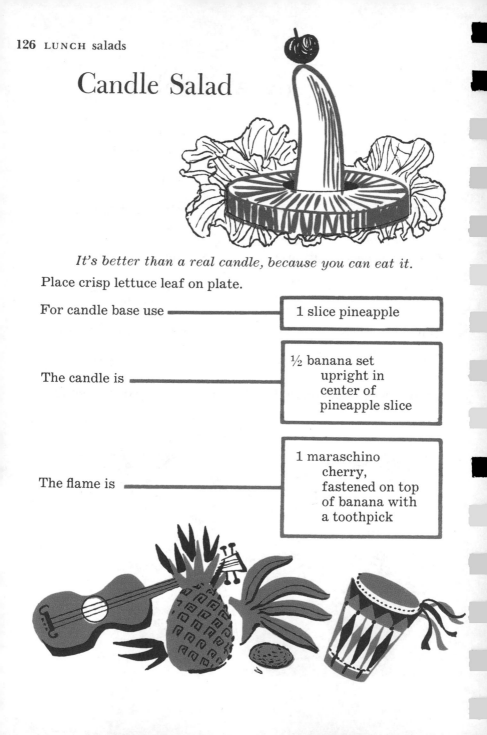

It's better than a real candle, because you can eat it.

Place crisp lettuce leaf on plate.

For candle base use —————— 1 slice pineapple

The candle is —————— ½ banana set upright in center of pineapple slice

The flame is —————— 1 maraschino cherry, fastened on top of banana with a toothpick

Bunny Salad

This bunny has just come out of the garden.

Place crisp lettuce leaf on plate.

On top of it, place upside down ———— | 1 chilled pear half |

Make bunny, using narrow
end for face.

Eyes ———————————— | 2 raisins |

Nose ———————————— | 1 red cinnamon candy |

Ears ———————————— | 2 blanched almonds |

For his tail ———————— | cottage cheese ball |

Potato Salad

Boil ══════════════════ | 4 medium potatoes |

(Use 2 quarts water, 1 teaspoon salt in covered pan. Cook 30 to 35 minutes, or until skins start to break and fork slips in easily.)

Drain off water, then cover with cold water, and drain again.

Lay potatoes on cutting board and pull off skin.

Put cold peeled potatoes in salad bowl. Break into bite-sized pieces with fork.

Add ══════════════ |
3 hard-cooked eggs, sliced (page 109)
1 cup diced celery
¼ cup minced onion
¼ cup pickle relish
¼ cup French dressing
|

Sprinkle in ══════════ | ¼ teaspoon salt |

Toss together and chill thoroughly.

Just before serving, fold in ══ |
½ cup cooked salad dressing or mayonnaise
|

Serve in lettuce-lined bowl. *6 servings.*

"I found out you can save time if you chop up the onion and celery while the potatoes are boiling." **Bette Anne**

Use a fork to break up potatoes in bowl.

Chop several stalks of celery at once.

Cut surface of onion in tiny squares. Cut across in tiny slices.

Toss salad gently with two forks.

Use a rubber scraper to fold in salad dressing.

Lay whole leaves of lettuce around the bowl to line it.

Whiz Nut Bread

Heat oven to 350°.

Grease thoroughly 9-inch loaf pan.

Mix in bowl —————

½ cup sugar
1 egg
1¼ cups milk
3 cups Bisquick

Beat hard 30 seconds. Batter may be lumpy.

Stir in —————

1½ cups chopped nuts

Pour into pan.

Bake *45 to 50 minutes,* until a toothpick stuck in center comes out clean.

Cool. Always slice with a bread knife.

"Betty Crocker said not to worry about a crack in your nut bread. It's supposed to be there."
Chris

Muffins

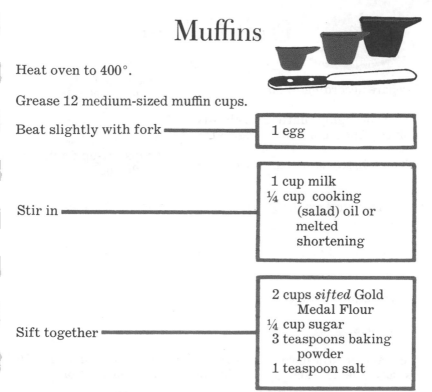

Heat oven to 400°.

Grease 12 medium-sized muffin cups.

Beat slightly with fork ———

> 1 egg

Stir in ———

> 1 cup milk
> ¼ cup cooking
>   (salad) oil or
>   melted
>   shortening

Sift together ———

> 2 cups *sifted* Gold
>   Medal Flour
> ¼ cup sugar
> 3 teaspoons baking
>   powder
> 1 teaspoon salt

Stir into milk mixture *just* until flour is moistened. Batter will be lumpy. Do not overmix. Fill muffin cups ⅔ full.

Bake *20 to 25 minutes,* or until golden brown.

Makes 12 medium-sized muffins.

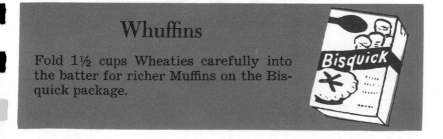

Whuffins

Fold 1½ cups Wheaties carefully into the batter for richer Muffins on the Bisquick package.

Fruit Gelatin

Prepare according to directions —

| 1 package fruit-flavored gelatin |

Stir thoroughly, until entirely dissolved. Then chill in refrigerator.

When mixture starts to thicken, add —

| 2 cups cut-up fruit, drained |

Pour into ring mold, square pan, or fancy mold if you have one. Chill until set.

Unmold by dipping quickly in hot water. Gelatin slips out easily.

Serve plain or with cream.

6 servings.

To make gelatin in colored layers as photographed on page 156 is easy. Just let each layer set before you add the next one.

Try Mixing Your Fruits

Bananas and strawberries are good together.

Raspberries and peaches are go-togethers, too, and canned pineapple with sweet cherries.

But never use fresh or frozen pineapple! It keeps the gelatin runny.

Applesauce

Wash, peel, quarter, and core ——— | 8 medium apples

Add water about ½-inch deep in pan. Cover tightly and bring to a boil (about 5 minutes). Turn down heat and simmer until tender.

Stir in to taste ——— | about ½ cup sugar

Reheat to boiling.

Sprinkle lightly with cinnamon or nutmeg and serve warm or cold.

Pink Applesauce

Add 2 or 3 drops of red food coloring or about a tablespoon of redhots.

"I just love pink applesauce. And it's easy!"   **Linda**

Whiz Applesauce Cake

Heat oven to 350°.

Grease and flour a 13-inch oblong pan.

Mix in bowl ————

> 1 package Betty Crocker Honey Spice Cake Mix
> ¼ teaspoon soda

Add ————

> ⅔ cup water

Beat vigorously for 2 minutes (300 strokes). An electric mixer can be used if you scrape the sides down often. Use medium speed.

Add ————

> 2 unbeaten eggs

Beat 1 minute.

Add ————

> ¾ cup thick applesauce

Beat 1 more minute (low speed on mixer).

Fold in ————

> ⅓ cup chopped nuts

Pour into prepared pan.

Bake *about 35 minutes*.

Cool. Ice with Easy Penuche Icing (page 24).

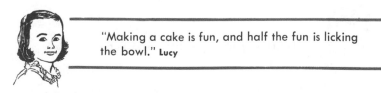

"Making a cake is fun, and half the fun is licking the bowl." **Lucy**

Shake flour in greased pan until bottom and sides are coated. Shake out excess flour.

Use shortening to grease the bottom and sides of the pan.

Use a rubber scraper on the sides of the mixing bowl.

Use a rubber scraper to fold nuts into the batter.

Backyard Picnic Lunch

Cold Sliced Ham
Potato Salad (page 128)
Dill Pickles   Picnic Buns
            (split and buttered)
Ice Cream Cones
Stir-n-Drop Oatmeal Cookies

Stir-n-Drop Oatmeal Cookies

Just about the best filler there is for the cooky jar.

Heat oven to 375°.

Combine in bowl
> 1 cup *sifted* Gold
>   Medal Flour
> 1 teaspoon baking
>   powder
> ½ teaspoon salt
> ½ teaspoon
>   cinnamon
> ½ teaspoon ginger
> 1 cup brown sugar
>   (packed)
> 1 cup rolled oats

Then mix in thoroughly
> ¼ cup cooking
>   (salad) oil
> 2 tablespoons milk
> 1 egg

Stir in
> ¾ cup Spanish
>   peanuts

Drop by rounded teaspoonfuls 2 inches apart on lightly greased baking sheet.

Bake *about 10 minutes,* just until soft.

Makes about 3 dozen cookies.

Butterscotch Brownies

Heat oven to 350°.

Grease an 8-inch square pan.

In saucepan melt over low heat —— | ¼ cup shortening

Take from heat and stir in —— | 1 cup light brown sugar (packed)

Set aside to cool.

Into cooled sugar and shortening stir◄ | 1 egg

Add and blend well —— | ¾ cup *sifted* Gold Medal Flour
1 teaspoon baking powder
½ teaspoon salt

Then stir in —— | ½ teaspoon vanilla
½ cup chopped nuts

Spread in pan.

Bake *25 minutes,* only until a toothpick stuck in center comes out clean. Do not overbake.

Cool in the pan and cut into squares.

Makes 16 2-inch squares.

"It's better to bake brownies not long enough than too long. Better ask mother to help you decide when these are done." **Betty Crocker**

Well-packed brown sugar will hold its shape when turned out of the cup.

There is a color photograph of Brownies, Coconut Macaroons, and Date Bars on page 160.

Whiz Coconut Macaroons

Whether chocolate or vanilla, they're made so quickly with Betty Crocker Coconut Macaroon Mix.

Whiz Date Bars

They have an oatmeal-coconut crust and rich date filling. Ready in a jiffy with Betty Crocker Date Bar Mix.

Brownies

Heat oven to 350°.

Grease an 8-inch square pan.

Put in mixing bowl —————————————

2 squares
unsweetened
chocolate
(2 ounces)
⅓ cup shortening

Set bowl in pan of hot water and heat to melt chocolate.

Take from heat and beat in ——————

1 cup sugar
2 eggs

Stir in ——————————————————

¾ cup *sifted* Gold
Medal Flour
½ teaspoon baking
powder
½ teaspoon salt

Then mix in ——————————————

½ cup chopped nuts

Spread in pan.

Bake *30 to 35 minutes,* only until a toothpick stuck in center comes out clean. Cool in pan, and cut in squares.

Makes 16 2-inch squares.

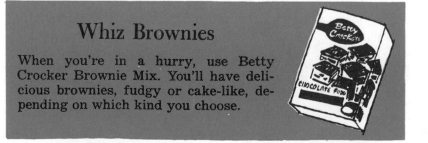

Whiz Brownies

When you're in a hurry, use Betty Crocker Brownie Mix. You'll have delicious brownies, fudgy or cake-like, depending on which kind you choose.

Dinner

Dinner is the sociable meal of the day when all the family sit down together and tell what's happened at school, at work, and at play.

You can help make dinner more than just another meal if you learn and practice the arts of the dinner table.

Take Pride in the Table. For happy family meals set the table just as carefully and attractively as you would for company. Always use a pretty centerpiece even if only a little pot of ivy from the window sill or a figurine off the cupboard shelf.

Care About Etiquette and Good Manners. When you have good manners people like you better and enjoy having you around. There is a reason for all the rules—to show consideration and thoughtfulness for others and make mealtimes a pleasure.

Good manners are not something to put on for company, but should be a part of us. They are like walking and talking and all other skills. Once we learn them, they just come naturally.

Make Dinner a Fun Time. Start a game of Table Topics. Each member of the family has a turn choosing the topic and all tell everything they know about it. Anyone may be challenged, so you'll want to keep the dictionary or encyclopedia handy.

Relishes

Fancy little extras like these always look tricky. But they're really easy, and fun to make.

Carrot Curls

Peel fresh crisp carrots with a peeler.

Slice the length of carrot paper-thin, with peeler, for long very thin slices.

Roll up each slice around your finger and hold it together with a toothpick. Be sure the shape is round. Soak curls in ice water for about an hour to hold their shape.

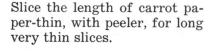

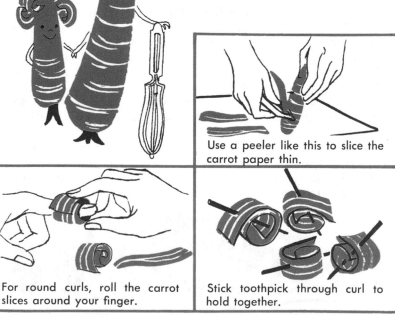

Use a peeler like this to slice the carrot paper thin.

For round curls, roll the carrot slices around your finger.

Stick toothpick through curl to hold together.

Celery Curls

Separate, then wash, a stalk of celery. Cut each rib into short lengths.

Slit in narrow strips at both ends. Soak in ice water until ends curl.

Cut several stalks of celery at once.

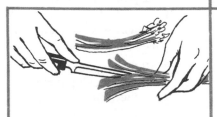

Slit both ends of the celery stick.

The finished celery curl looks like this.

Radish Roses

Scrub fresh red radishes.

Cut off root end. Leave a bit of stem and leaf.

Then cut *thin* "petals" around radish from root end almost to stem end.

Place "roses" in ice water to "blossom."

Use a small paring knife to make "petals" on radishes.

Ice water makes the radish rose open its petals.

Italian Spaghetti

*Aren't you glad you don't have to go
to Italy to get this favorite dish?*

Heat in heavy frying pan —— ¼ cup cooking (salad) oil

Add and brown —— 1 pound ground beef

Add and cook until yellow ——
2 tablespoons minced parsley
2 medium onions, chopped
2 cloves garlic, minced

Add ——
two 8-ounce cans tomato puree
two 6-ounce cans tomato paste
2 teaspoons Worcestershire sauce
salt to taste

Simmer over low heat 2 hours.

Follow directions on package for cooking —— 8 ounces long spaghetti

Pour sauce over spaghetti and sprinkle with grated Parmesan cheese.

6 servings.

Meat Loaf

Heat oven to 350°

Combine in bowl ————

> 3 slices soft bread, broken in pieces
> 1 cup milk
> 1 egg
> 1¼ teaspoons salt
> ¼ cup minced onion
> 1 tablespoon Worcestershire sauce

Stir together thoroughly.

Mix in ————

> 1½ pounds ground beef or meat loaf mixture

Form into loaf and place in 9-inch loaf pan.

Bake *1 hour.*

6 to 8 servings.

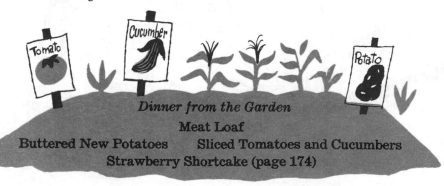

Dinner from the Garden

Meat Loaf

Buttered New Potatoes   Sliced Tomatoes and Cucumbers

Strawberry Shortcake (page 174)

Things You Can Do
with Meat Loaf

Hot Topper

Spread 3 tablespoons catsup or chili sauce over top of loaf before baking.

Tuckaway

When forming loaf, tuck in 3 hard-cooked eggs along the center.

Frosted

When loaf is baked, frost the top with mashed potatoes. Sprinkle with paprika and broil until golden.

Baby Beefies

Shape meat loaf mixture into 8 small loaves and lay in shallow pan. Top each baby loaf with a thin slice of onion. Bake at 350° for 1 hour.

> "Meat loaf that's left over makes the most wonderful sandwiches!" **Becky**

Swedish Meat Balls

A wonderful way to dress up ground beef.

Melt in frying pan	1 tablespoon butter

Add and cook until tender	1 green pepper, chopped 1 onion, minced

Stir in	one 10½-ounce can condensed chicken with rice soup one 10½-ounce can condensed tomato soup 1 cup water or beef stock

Heat to boiling, then turn down heat.

While sauce cooks, make meat balls.

Put in bowl	2 slices soft bread, broken in pieces ¼ cup evaporated milk 1 egg 1 teaspoon salt 1 pound ground beef

Mix thoroughly and shape into balls about the size of a ping pong ball. Drop balls into simmering sauce and cook slowly about 1 hour, or until sauce has cooked down enough to be thickened.

6 servings.

Drop the meat balls in carefully so that the hot sauce won't splatter.

Chili Concoction

You serve this in bowls and eat it with a spoon and you never tasted such good chili.

Melt in frying pan —————— 2 tablespoons fat

Add ———————— 1½ pounds ground beef

Break meat apart and stir with fork as it browns lightly.

Then stir in ——————
one no. 2 can
   tomatoes
one no. 2 can
   kidney beans
1 large onion,
   chopped
1 tablespoon chili
   powder
½ teaspoon salt

Heat to boiling,
then turn down heat.

Simmer 1 hour.

4 to 6 servings.

Spanish Rice

Follow directions on
package for cooking ————

1 cup rice

Heat oven to 400°

Fry until crisp on medium heat ———

4 slices bacon, cut up

Put bacon in 1½-quart baking dish
and toss it around to grease dish.

Add to bacon fat ————

¼ cup minced onion ¼ cup chopped green pepper

Cook until onion is yellow.

Add (in frying pan) ————

cooked rice (3 cups) 2 cups canned tomatoes 1½ teaspoons salt

Turn into baking dish.

Sprinkle over top ————

¼ cup grated cheese

Bake *25 to 30 minutes.*

4 to 6 servings.

Lay bacon flat on board to cut across in narrow strips.

American Pizza

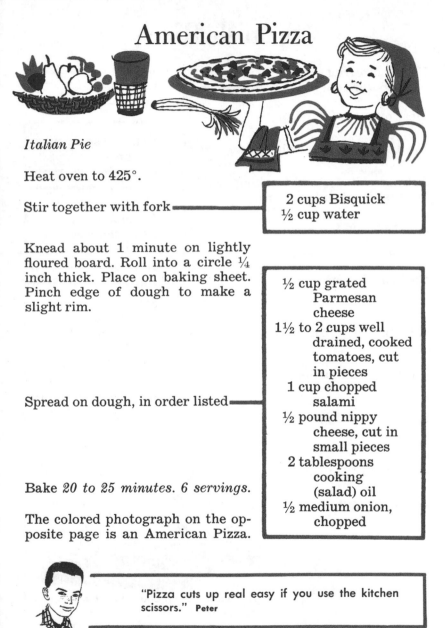

Italian Pie

Heat oven to 425°.

Stir together with fork————

> 2 cups Bisquick
> ½ cup water

Knead about 1 minute on lightly floured board. Roll into a circle ¼ inch thick. Place on baking sheet. Pinch edge of dough to make a slight rim.

Spread on dough, in order listed————

> ½ cup grated Parmesan cheese
> 1½ to 2 cups well drained, cooked tomatoes, cut in pieces
> 1 cup chopped salami
> ½ pound nippy cheese, cut in small pieces
> 2 tablespoons cooking (salad) oil
> ½ medium onion, chopped

Bake *20 to 25 minutes. 6 servings.*

The colored photograph on the opposite page is an American Pizza.

"Pizza cuts up real easy if you use the kitchen scissors." **Peter**

Long John Silver Sandwich

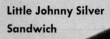
Little Johnny Silver Sandwich

Fruit Gelatin (see page 132)

Strawberry Minute Pie (see page 176)

Strawberry Shortcake (see page 174)

Raggedy Ann Salad (see page 125)

Three Men in a Boat (see page 123)

Buttered Green Beans

Wash and snip ends of 1½ pounds green beans. Lay beans on cutting board and cut in 1-inch lengths.

In covered saucepan heat about 1 inch salted water to boiling.

Add beans and bring to boil, then turn down heat and cook slowly about 15 minutes or until tender.

Drain any extra water and add 1 tablespoon butter.

4 servings.

Cut several beans at one time.

"We do carrots and cabbage this way at our house with just a little bit of water. And they're so good!" Eric

Corn on the Cob

Just before cooking, remove husks and silks.

In covered saucepan, heat about 1 inch water to boiling.

Put a few inner husks on the bottom of the pan and lay corn on top. Cook *3 to 6 minutes,* depending on the size and age of the corn.

A little sugar helps the flavor of older corn.

Frozen Vegetables

They look and taste just like fresh vegetables. So quick and easy because they are all cleaned and ready to cook. Follow package directions.

Cook the exact time given on the package. Start counting the minutes when the frozen block of vegetables is broken up and the water starts boiling again.

Use high heat until steam appears, then turn down heat and simmer until tender.

Canned Peas De Luxe

Pour liquid from can of peas into saucepan. Boil it, uncovered, until liquid cooks down. Add 1 tablespoon butter. Put peas in pan and heat.

The liquid from the can makes the flavor of the peas better.

Cabbage Wedgies

Remove outer leaves of medium-sized cabbage head.

Put on cutting board and cut in half, storing one half for Cole Slaw (page 168) the next day.

Turn flat side down and cut in half again.

Then cut each piece in half, giving you four wedges.

Cook, covered, in ½ to 1 inch boiling salted water, bringing water to a rolling boil then turning heat low and cooking about 15 minutes, until tender.

Prick with a fork to test.

Drain off extra cooking water and add 1 tablespoon butter. Turn wedges so they are all buttered.

Serve a wedge to each person. Sprinkle with paprika for color.

4 servings.

TV Dinner on Trays
Spanish Rice (page 151)
Pickles and Relishes
Whuffins (page 131)
Apple Crisp (page 171)

This is how you cut the cabbage in wedges.

Boiled Potatoes

Scrub thoroughly or peel thin. Cook covered in 1 inch boiling, salted water until potatoes are tender. It takes about 30 minutes, depending on size of potatoes. Prick with fork to tell when tender.

Drain.

Shake over low heat to dry.

Serve with butter, salt, and pepper . . . and a sprinkling of parsley if you like.

Mashed Potatoes

Peel and quarter ——————— | 6 medium potatoes |

In covered pan heat about 1 inch salted water to boiling. Add potatoes and bring to boil, then turn down heat and cook slowly about 20 minutes, until potatoes are tender when pricked with a fork. Drain remaining water or boil dry.

Mash with potato masher or electric mixer.

Add ——————— | ½ cup hot milk
3 tablespoons butter
¼ teaspoon salt |

Beat until light and fluffy.

6 servings.

"Betty Crocker says when you boil the potatoes in their jackets, they taste better and they're more good for you, too." **Randee**

Baked Potatoes

Heat oven to 400°.

Choose baking potatoes of medium size. Scrub with a brush.

Rub with fat for soft skin.

Prick skin with fork to let steam escape during baking.

Bake until potatoes are tender (prick with fork to test) about 1 hour.

To serve plain baked potatoes, cut criss-cross gash on potato tops.

Squeeze until potato pops up through opening.

Season with salt, pepper, and butter and serve at once.

Mother's Day Special

Swedish Meat Balls (page 148)
Baked Potatoes
Sunshine Salad (page 169)
Strawberry Ice Cream
Heart Cake (page 30)

Potatoes Anna

Raw-fried potatoes with glamor.

Melt 2 tablespoons butter in heavy frying pan.

Peel very thin 4 medium-sized potatoes, and cut in paper-thin slices.

Arrange slices in two or three layers in frying pan. Sprinkle each layer with salt and dot with butter.

Cover tightly and heat until steaming. Then turn down heat and cook 15 minutes.

Uncover. Cook until the bottom is crispy brown.

Turn potatoes out upside down onto serving plate.

4 servings.

Paper-thin slices cook faster.

You may overlap your potatoes a little, but each layer should be only one slice thick.

Put a plate over the pan and then turn the pan upside down so that the brown crust will be on the top.

Scalloped Potatoes

Use small bits of butter for dotting.

Heat oven to 350°.

In 1½-quart baking dish arrange in two layers ——————

| 3 to 4 cups peeled, thinly sliced raw potatoes 1 tablespoon minced onion |

Sprinkle each layer with salt and dot with ——————

| 2 to 4 tablespoons butter |

Pour over all ——————

| 1¼ cups hot milk |

Bake uncovered *about 1¼ hours.*

4 servings.

Cole Slaw

Call it cabbage salad and it will taste just as good.

Shred on cutting board ————

> ½ medium head
> cabbage

Chill in plastic bag in refrigerator
to crisp.

Combine in salad bowl ————

> 1 medium onion,
> minced
> 2 tablespoons
> vinegar
> ¼ cup evaporated
> milk or heavy
> cream
> ¼ cup salad dressing
> ¼ teaspoon salt
> ½ teaspoon dry
> mustard

Add cabbage and toss together.

Sprinkle with paprika.

Serve icy cold.

6 servings.

Dad's Birthday Dinner
Hamburgers (page 104)
Scalloped Potatoes (page 167) Cole Slaw
Brown 'N Serve Rolls
Velvet Fudge Cake (page 178)
Ice Cream

Sunshine Salad

Empty into small mixing bowl —— 1 package lemon-
flavored gelatin

Stir in ———— 1 cup boiling water

Stir thoroughly until gelatin is
entirely dissolved.

Then stir in ———— ½ cup ice water
one 9-ounce can
crushed
pineapple
pinch of salt

Chill in refrigerator.

When gelatin starts to thicken, add — 2 medium-sized
carrots, grated

Pour into 8-inch square pan and chill in refrigerator until firm.

Cut in squares and serve on crisp lettuce leaves with mayonnaise.

6 servings.

Hold your fingers away from
the grater.

Use a knife to cut salad in
squares.

Drop Biscuits

Heat oven to 450°.

Grease baking sheet lightly.

Mix in bowl ———————

> 2 cups *sifted* Gold
>   Medal Flour
> 3 teaspoons baking
>   powder
> 1 teaspoon salt

With blender cut in until fine ———

> ⅓ cup soft
>   shortening

With fork stir in ———————

> ¾ cup milk

Drop biscuit-sized pieces of dough onto baking sheet. (Push the dough off the fork with rubber scraper.)

Leave 2-inch space between biscuits so they can brown and will be separate.

Bake *10 to 12 minutes,* until brown. Serve piping hot.

Makes 12 to 20 biscuits.

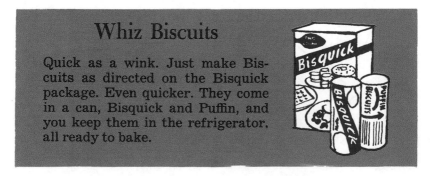

Whiz Biscuits

Quick as a wink. Just make Biscuits as directed on the Bisquick package. Even quicker. They come in a can, Bisquick and Puffin, and you keep them in the refrigerator, all ready to bake.

Apple Crisp

A real family dessert. Especially good on a cold winter night.

Heat oven to 350°.

Spread in 8-inch square pan ——— | 4 cups sliced apples |

Sprinkle with mixture of ———

¼ cup water
1 teaspoon cinnamon
½ teaspoon salt

Work together until crumbly, using pastry blender ———

1 cup sugar
¾ cup *sifted* Gold Medal Flour
⅓ cup soft butter

Spread crumb mixture over apples.

Bake uncovered *about 40 minutes.*

Serve warm with rich milk.

6 servings.

The apples should be spread evenly in the pan.

It's easy to cut in shortening when you use a pastry blender.

Hot Fudge Pudding

Heat oven to 350°.

Blend in bowl ——————
> 1 cup *sifted* Gold
>   Medal Flour
> 2 teaspoons
>   baking powder
> ¼ teaspoon salt
> ¾ cup sugar
> 2 tablespoons
>   cocoa

Stir in ——————
> ½ cup milk
> 2 tablespoons
>   cooking
>   (salad) oil
> 1 cup chopped nuts

Spread in 9-inch square pan.

In small bowl blend ——————
> 1 cup brown sugar
>   (packed)
> ¼ cup cocoa

Sprinkle sugar mixture over top of batter.

Pour over all —————— 1¾ cups hot water

Bake *45 minutes*.

Serve warm or cold with rich milk or cream.

9 servings.

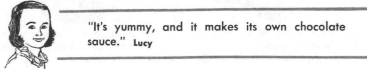

"It's yummy, and it makes its own chocolate sauce." **Lucy**

You will get a more even topping if you use a flour sifter to sprinkle the brown sugar and cocoa mixture.

Use a rubber scraper to spread batter in pan.

Strawberry Shortcake

The All-American dessert. Now you can enjoy it the year around, with fresh or frozen berries.

Heat oven to 450°.

Grease two 8-inch layer pans.

Stir together in a bowl ——
2 cups *sifted* Gold Medal Flour
2 tablespoons sugar
3 teaspoons baking powder
1 teaspoon salt

With pastry blender, cut in fine ——
⅓ cup shortening

Stir in, with fork, just until blended ——
1 cup milk

Spread dough in pans. Dot with butter.

Bake *about 15 minutes,* until medium brown.

Place one layer on serving plate upside down; cover with sweetened berries; top with other layer, right side up; cover with more berries.

Serve warm with plain or whipped cream.

6 to 8 servings.

If you like, you can make small shortcakes like the one photographed on page 157.

It's easier to mix the dry ingredients with a fork.

A pastry blender is best for cutting in shortening.

Use a rubber scraper to spread the dough, then dot on small bits of butter.

The berries stay on the cake better if you turn the bottom layer upside down.

Whiz Strawberry Shortcake

The jiffy kind. Just make it as directed on the Bisquick package.

Bisquick

Strawberry Minute Pie

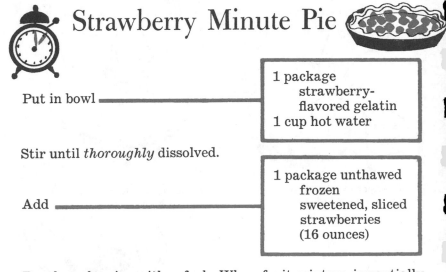

Put in bowl ——————

> 1 package
>   strawberry-
>   flavored gelatin
> 1 cup hot water

Stir until *thoroughly* dissolved.

Add ——————

> 1 package unthawed
>   frozen
>   sweetened, sliced
>   strawberries
>   (16 ounces)

Break up berries with a fork. When fruit mixture is partially set pour into a cooled, baked pie shell.

Chill in refrigerator until filling is set.

Just before serving top with whipped cream or ice cream.

Whiz Cream Puffs

Now you can make your own, easily, with Betty Crocker Cream Puff Mix. Fill them with ice cream, whipped cream, or your favorite pudding mix. Crushed strawberries mixed with the whipped cream makes a good filling too.

Whiz Pie Shell

Always tender and flaky. Just make the baked pie shell as directed on the package of Betty Crocker Instant Pie Crust Mix in sticks.

Velvet Crumb Cake

Heat oven to 350°.

Grease and flour 8-inch square pan.

Stir together ——————

| 1⅓ cups Bisquick |
| ¾ cup sugar |

Add ——————

| 3 tablespoons soft shortening |
| 1 egg |
| ¼ cup milk |

Beat vigorously 1 minute.

Stir in ——————

| ½ cup more milk |
| 1 teaspoon vanilla |

Beat ½ minute more.

Pour into pan.

Bake *35 to 40 minutes.*

While cake is still warm cover with Broiled Coconut Icing.

Broiled Coconut Icing

Mix  ——————

| 3 tablespoons soft butter |
| ⅓ cup brown sugar (packed) |
| 2 tablespoons top milk |
| ½ cup flaked coconut |
| ¼ cup chopped nuts |

Spread mixture over warm cake in pan. Place 3 inches under broiler at low heat until mixture bubbles and browns (3 to 5 minutes). Watch the icing closely as it broils, so it won't burn.

Velvet Fudge Cake

*There's a rich, gooey frosting
baked in the middle and on top.*

Heat oven to 350°.

Grease and flour 8-inch square pan.

Stir together ———————

> 1⅓ cups Bisquick
> ¾ cup sugar
> ⅓ cup cocoa

Add ———————

> 3 tablespoons soft
>   shortening
> 1 egg
> ¼ cup milk

Beat vigorously 1 minute.

Stir in ———————

> ½ cup more milk
> 1 teaspoon vanilla

Beat ½ minute more.

Pour half of batter into pan. Spread with half of Topping
(below).

Cover with remaining batter.

Bake *35 to 40 minutes.*

Immediately spread with rest of Topping. Serve warm.

For Topping, mix ½ cup (½ package) semi-sweet chocolate
pieces, melted, ⅓ cup water, 2 cups finely chopped coconut.

Rules

IT PAYS TO BE CAREFUL

Pot holders save you from burns.

Pans won't upset and spill if handles are turned to back of range.

Ask your mother before you use a sharp knife or the can opener.

When you use the vegetable peeler, cut away from yourself.

Slice, dice, chop, and mince on a chopping board.

FOR PREPARATION

Vegetable peeler

Vegetable brush

Grater

Cutting board

Knife for chopping

Wire strainer

Can opener

Ring mold

FOR COOKING

Saucepan

Double boiler

Pancake turner

Heavy frying pan

A Good Cook Measures Exactly

Flour — Sift more than you need onto a square of waxed paper or into a bowl. Spoon lightly into cup, heaping it up. Level off. Don't shake or tap cup.

Sugar — White granulated and confectioners'— Spoon lightly into cup. Level off. Don't knock or tap cup.
Brown—Fill cup and press down with your fingers. Pack it in until sugar holds its shape when you turn it out.

Salt — Pour salt into small glass or bowl and dip into it to measure. You may not get the right amount if you pour it into your spoon.

Baking Powder — Stir, then fill measuring spoon. Level off.

Vanilla — Pour into measuring spoon from bottle, not over your mixing bowl. You might pour in too much.

Shortening — Take small amounts with rubber scraper and pack into cup. Level off.

Butter — For approximate measure:
There are 8 tablespoons or ½ cup in each ¼ pound stick and 4 tablespoons or ¼ cup in half a stick.

Liquids — Set glass measuring cup on table. Pour in liquid to proper mark.

You'll Need These Utensils

FOR MIXING

Kitchen fork and knife

Pastry blender

Wooden spoon

Rotary egg beater or electric mixer

Mixing bowls

Rubber scraper

FOR MEASURING

Graduated Measuring Cups—¼, ⅓, ½, 1 cup.

Liquid Measuring Cup

Measuring Spoons ¼, ½, 1 tsp., 1 tbsp.

Straight-edged Knife

Sifter

Rubber Scraper

FOR BAKING

Baking sheet

Pie pan

8-inch square pan

9-inch loaf pan

13-inch oblong pan

Two 8 or 9-inch round layer pans

12-cup muffin pan

Wide spatula

Rolling pin with cover

Cutters

Pastry cloth

Wire rack

You'll Want to Know These Cooking Terms

Bake—Cook in oven.

Beat—Mix vigorously, over and over with a spoon or fork or round and round with a beater.

Blend—Combine two or more ingredients well.

Boil—Cook in liquid so hot that it bubbles and keeps on bubbling.

Broil—Cook next to heat, under broiler in range or over coals.

Chop—Cut in pieces with knife or chopper.

Combine—Mix together.

Cube—Cut in ¼ to ½-inch squares of six equal sides.

Cut In—Combine shortening and flour with pastry blender.

Dice—Cut in very small ¼-inch squares.

Dot—Drop bits of butter or cheese here and there over food.

Drain—Pour off liquid.

Flour—Dust greased pans with flour until well coated on bottom and sides. Shake out extra flour.

Fold—Combine gently, bringing rubber scraper down through mixture, across bottom, up and over top until blended.

Grease—Spread bottom and sides of pan with shortening.

Knead—Work dough with your hands in a folding-back and pressing-forward motion.

Melt—Heat until liquid.

Mince—Chop in tiny pieces.

Roll Out—Place on board and spread thin with a rolling pin.

Shred—Cut in very thin strips.

Sift—Put through a flour sifter or fine sieve.

Simmer—Cook over heat near boiling but not hot enough to bubble.

Soft Shortening—Butter, lard, or vegetable shortening at room temperature, so it can be measured easily.

Stir—Mix round and round with spoon.

Toss—Mix lightly.

Whip—Add air by beating with beater or electric mixer.

Kitchen Manners

BEFORE YOU START TO COOK

Choose a time to suit your mother, so you won't be in her way.

Wear an apron to keep your dress or blue jeans clean and be sure to wash your hands.

Read your recipe and all directions very carefully. Look at the pictures. They tell you how to do each step.

Put all your ingredients on a tray. Then set each one off as you use it.

On another tray put all the tools and pans you'll need.

WHEN YOU'RE THROUGH

Have you left anything out? Read your recipe again and be sure.

Is everything spic and span? Then your mother will be glad to have you cook again.

INDEX

ENJOY YOUR COOKBOOK TODAY

We're excited to bring you this treasured edition of *Betty Crocker's Cook Book for Boys and Girls*. All the recipes are exactly as they appeared in the original 1957 book to reflect the heritage of American cooking and baking. Eating habits may have changed, but the fond memories of making the recipes from this cookbook remain the same.

Some ingredients are no longer available. You may want to ask an adult what ingredients to use so you can make these recipes and they will still taste as good today! Food safety concerns have also changed over the years. We no longer can enjoy recipes using raw eggs that aren't cooked or baked. However, today we can substitute pasteurized eggs and safely enjoy these recipes. You can find cartons of pasteurized eggs in the refrigerator section of the grocery store. Or use a pasteurized fat-free cholesterol-free egg product. It is available in cartons in the refrigerator or freezer section of your grocery store.

Please use only pasteurized eggs or pasteurized egg product in the following two recipes:

Peanut Butter Cremes (page 57): Use 1 pasteurized egg or 1/4 cup fat-free cholesterol-free egg product for the 1 egg.

Eggnog (page 61): Use 1 pasteurized egg or 1/4 cup fat-free cholesterol-free egg product for the 1 egg.